A Bustle & Sew Publication

Copyright © Bustle & Sew Limited 2013

The right of Helen Dickson to be identified as the author of this work has been asserted in accordance with the Copyright, Designs and Patents Act 1988.

Every effort has been made to ensure that all the information in this book is accurate. However, due to differing conditions, tools and individual skills, the publisher cannot be responsible for any injuries, losses and other damages that may result from the use of the information in this book.

ISBN-13: 978-1494431211
ISBN-10: 1494431211
First published 2013 by:
Bustle & Sew
Coombe Leigh
Chillington
Kingsbridge
Devon TQ7 2LE
UK

www.bustleandsew.com

Hello,

And welcome to the December 2013 issue of the Bustle & Sew Magazine. Another year is drawing to a close, but there's still plenty of fun to look forward to in this month's issue. I've designed all the Christmas patterns to give the best results - but without taking too much time - I know what a busy time of year this can be!

But if you'd like a little slow stitching to enjoy while taking a break from the seasonal rush, then do check out my Mr Fox: Wish Upon a Star pattern - which comes with its very own video tutorial - my first ever as part of a pattern.

It's hard to believe that this time last year Ben and I were counting down the days until the arrival of his baby sister! Daisy is one now, and such a big part of our family, it's hard to imagine how ~~boring~~ peaceful life was without her! This year she'll be sure to want to join in the fun whether it's the traditional Parlour games on page 32 or stealing the camel from the Nativity Set on page 37!

So, wherever you are, and however you're spending your holidays, I'd like to wish you a very happy, healthy and peaceful Christmas.

Best wishes

Helen, Ben and Daisy xxx

Contents

Christmas is fast approaching, and we're all eagerly anticipating all the festive traditions that surround this most wonderful of holidays. A warm glow comes over my home as I light festive candles and bring holly, ivy and other evergreens gathered from woods and hedgerows, into the home and later - the Christmas tree. The fragrance of pine, cinnamon and oranges fills the air as I bake mince pies, ice my chocolate log whilst listening to carols on my trusty kitchen radio.

Batson Creek near Salcombe

Although living in the countryside has its drawbacks in winter, mud, lack of local facilities (in January I'll have to travel nearly 30 miles to our local hospital for my long-awaited knee op), in my opinion these are more than compensated for by the wonderful coast and countryside around me, and the friendly community in which I live. I have only to move from beside my log burner and step outside to enjoy crisp, fresh walks through our woods where I'm sure to meet other dog-walkers for a friendly chat, or along the now mainly deserted beach where Ben and Daisy can romp and play without a care in the world. (CLICK HERE for a little bit of sedate (Ben) and splashy (Daisy) swimming at Batson Creek on a still frosty morning)

Our village really springs into life at Christmas. We have the Pensioners' Christmas party, carol singing (complete with band) around our Christmas tree, the Candlelit Carol Service at St Michael's Church in Stokenham - where Rosie and Dan will be getting married this year - as well as a host of other events. I'm wondering whether to attend the Christmas wreath-making workshop in the Parish Hall, or possibly the great Stir-Up Sunday gathering - or maybe even both!! Then there's the Pantomime - another great Christmas tradition. This year it's Puss in Boots. Rosie and I both know Puss so we're off to support her and the rest of the Dartmouth Players after Christmas - it's even more fun when you know someone in the production! "Oh yes it is!!"

Merry Christmas everyone!!

Christmas Hare Card Hanger

A Nordic heart and winter hare - nice and cosy in his woolly scarf - could there possibly be any nicer way to display your cards this Christmas (great for all those Valentine tributes too !!).

Finished hare and heart measures 8" from the point of the heart to the tip of the hare's ears.

You will need:

- 12" x 7" stripey non-stretch fabric for heart

- 5" x 4" grey/blue felt for large heart applique

- 2" x 1 ½" scrap red felt for small heart applique

- 8" x 6" grey marl felt for hare

- Tiny scrap pale pink felt for hare's ear

- 6" x ½" felt/felted woollen for hare's scarf

- Stranded cotton embroidery floss in grey to match the hare's body, a darker grey, grey/blue to match large heart applique, black, pale pink and ecru

- 24" x 2" beige cotton twill tape

- 36" x ½" Christmas ribbon

- Toy stuffing

- Pinking shears (optional)

- Temporary fabric marker pen

- Small pegs for your cards

Notes: the template is given actual size. Use two strands of floss throughout.

Make your hare:

- Cut out two hare shapes. Place right sides outwards and join all around the bottom edge,

ie from nose tip to tail using a half cross stitch and matching grey floss. Then return the other way to complete the cross stitch.

- Lightly stuff the legs at this point using tiny pieces of toy stuffing - a stuffing stick is a really useful tool to push them into place. To make your stuffing stick simply break the point off a bamboo skewer and fray the end - this will "grab" the stuffing and you'll be able to push it into the hardest to reach places. It's best to stuff the legs now as it will be hard to do them nicely once you've stitched the rest of the body.

- Now stitch around the head and ears and again stuff the nose and ears before continuing along the back. Stuffing as you go and moulding with your hands for a nice smooth shape finish stitching around the hare's body.

- Cut the ear shape and attach to the ear with pale pink floss, using small straight stitches worked at right angles to the applique shape.

- Using the template as a guide draw in the lines for the back legs with your temporary fabric marker pen and back stitch with the dark grey floss going right through to the back of the hare and pulling quite tightly to indicate his nicely rounded legs.

- With black floss stitch his nose and eye with small straight stitches. Again go right through to the back for his eye and pull tightly to add contours to his face.

- Cut fringes about ½" into each short end of your scarf piece, then wrap around your hare's neck and secure with small stitches. Secure to his body as though it was being blown out behind him as he runs. (see photograph).

- Your hare is now complete.

Make your heart:

- Cut out two large heart shapes in your stripey fabric using pinking shears if you have them. Place one heart to the side for now.

- Cut a large heart in blue felt and small in red felt and applique to the right side of your stripey heart using small straight stitches at right angles to the edge of the shape. Use matching floss for the blue heart and ecru for the red heart. Work an 8 point star in the centre of the red heart using ecru floss.

- With your temporary fabric marker pen draw the leaf and vine design onto the blue felt heart following the template as a guide. This doesn't have to be an exact copy - just concentrate on nice smooth curves and scatter a few leaves and berries around! Stitch your leaf and vine design in ecru floss using stem stitch for the vine and satin stitch for the leaves and berries.

- Cut a 24" length of your Christmas ribbon and place it on top of your 2" twill tape, then stitch it into place down the middle of the twill tape.

- Make a sandwich placing the back of your heart wrong side up on a clean flat surface, then the cotton twill tape at the bottom of the point (see above) and then the front of the heart right side up. Pin or baste together, then machine around the edge leaving a 1 ½" gap on one side for stuffing. Stuff and then topstitch the gap closed. Cut an inverted "V" shape at the bottom of your ribbon/twill to prevent fraying - and it looks nice too!

- Stitch the hare to the top of the heart as shown in the photographs, and then stitch the remaining Christmas ribbon to the back of the hare to form a hanging loop.

- Peg cards to twill/ribbon using tiny pegs.

A Seaside Artist

An interview with designer and illustrator Jacqui Bignell

On the beach at Bigbury with husband Clive

Jacqui is not only a talented artist and designer, she and her husband Clive are also very dear friends of mine. The next two patterns in this issue, the Sparkle Reindeer and Wish Upon a Star: Mr Fox are based on Jacqui's line drawings, and so I thought you might like to "meet" her properly. Jacqui is inspired by country and seaside living and the rhythm of the changing seasons here in south Devon. Her passion for drawing and creating has lead her to establish her own business, Flapdoodledesigns, offering commssioned artwork as well as printable scrapbooking designs.

An illustration for "Simple Stitchery" by Bustle & Sew – Fly Stitch!

What do you love most about living here in south Devon?

I love living near the sea and the countryside. Every morning I walk my dog Lionel down the marsh to the estuary. We normally walk with three other people and we have seven dogs between us all running and playing in the open space. We often see a pair of herons, who don't seem to be at all bothered by our dogs, several different types of ducks, geese, swans and egrets. The wild flowers are beautiful and encourage butterflies whilst the hedgerow is full of blackberries and sloes in the autumn.

And about your own home?

The view (that's our view below!). We bought this house three years ago because we fell in love with the amazing view of the farm land, marsh and estuary. It is forever changing and in the evening we see the lights of Salcombe twinkling too. I love to watch the tractors ploughing with the seagulls swooping around them.

Lionel

flapdoodledesigns

The shepherds

Oxford

And what, in your opinion, makes the perfect country home?

A country home should be warm, cosy and practical. We have a woodburner and it's the best thing about winter. We do have to fight with the cat and the dog for space in front of it though!

Where do you find your inspiration?

The wild flowers around me and the animals and birds I see. I love gardening, although my garden is small it is packed with plants, I can never resist a bargain. I often take my camera with me photograph the wild flowers so that I can paint them when I'm home. My new autumn paintings are of toadstools and blackberries. There are so many different types of toadstool, some of them so delicate and beautiful. There are many of them growing in the marsh this time of year.

Please tell us about your favourite local shop….

The Harbour Bookshop in Kingsbridge is my favourite shop. It is a small independent bookshop with friendly knowledgeable staff, always willing to recommend books they have enjoyed. They even have a monthly newsletter in which they all review several books they have read. I could spend hours in there choosing books for myself and friends.

And your favourite local restaurant?

The Queens arms in the village of Slapton near to the sea at Start Bay. It is an old pub with oak beams and a warming open fire in the winter. We have been going there for years, when our children were younger they used to enjoy choosing games to play from the games cupboard whilst waiting for their food. The food is traditional pub food using locally produced vegetables, fish and meat and always served by friendly staff.

Describe your perfect weekend ….

When my children are home from university, after a lazy start we take our dog Lionel to a local beach, Lannacombe, my husband and son insist we take a football too. In the evening we get together with the rest of our family at either our house or my sister in laws.

On Sundays we like to go to Gara Rock for a walk on the beach, leaving my dad and mother in law in the Gara Rock Hotel at the top of the cliff (the walk down is very steep and strenuous) reading their newspapers and drinking coffee. After enjoying tea ourselves it's all back to our house for an early evening roast dinner.

Lookout hut at Gara Rock

Thank you to Jacqui for talking to us .. And also for the drawings for the next two patterns - as well as your Stitching Fox for the cover of my next pattern collection ….

And finally, how will you be celebrating Christmas this year?

Although they are 19 and 21 our children still enjoy opening their stockings on the end of our bed. We then open presents with my dad, who will be stating with us.

About midday we head off to my sister in laws to spend the rest of the day with her family. This year there will be eleven of us and a bump, my niece is expecting her second child in January. Sharing our Christmas dinner will be three dogs and my sister in laws cat. We then enjoy playing silly games whilst my elderly dad and mother in law fall asleep in front of the fire.

Keep in touch with Jacqui over on her Facebook page:

www.facebook.com/flapdoodledesigns

If you'd like to commission your own original artwork - or maybe a line drawing for your own embroidery project, then you can contact Jacqui either on her Facebook page or by email:

White Christmas

Sparkle Reindeer Picture

Simple hand and machine applique - lots of vintage buttons and some sparkling battery-operated LED Christmas Lights make these two little reindeer from Flapdoodledesigns simply sparkle for Christmas!

Finished picture measures 16" square and is mounted on an artist's canvas block to be able to fix LED lights from the back.

You will need:

- 20" square medium weight non-stretchy fabric for background
- 12" x 7" brown tweedy fabric or felt for front reindeer
- 4" x 5" brown tweedy fabric or felt for back reindeer
- 8" square light brown felt for antlers
- 14 x 1 ½" square scraps of brightly coloured felt for letters
- 14 x 1 ½" square scraps of quilting weight cotton fabric for letters
- 10 x assorted ½" and ¾" vintage buttons for ornaments on antlers
- 2 x ½" pink buttons for cheeks (optional)
- 7 x ¼" white or cream buttons for spots on front reindeer (optional)

(if you can't find the pink or white buttons, then simply stitch these features in pink and white floss and satin stitch)

- Bondaweb
- Black, red, green and white stranded cotton embroidery floss - also in shades to match the fabric you choose for your reindeer and their antlers.
- Gold machine thread
- Set of 20 battery-operated LED lights - the sort with very small bulbs measuring about ⅛" across
- 66" x ¾" wide red velvet ribbon

- Temporary fabric marker pen
- Pinking shears (optional)
- Hot glue gun
- Staple gun
- Embroidery scissors/knitting needle or other sharp pointed object (to make holes for lights)
- Temporary fabric spray adhesive
- Embroidery foot for your sewing machine

Applique:

Notes:

The templates are given actual size, but you will need to join the pieces together (it should be obvious how they fit) and also add another couple of inches of reindeer body to the bottom - simple curves - just check the photograph and you'll see how they go.

Please also note the templates are given reversed for easy tracing onto the paper side of your Bondaweb.

- Place your canvas block in the centre of your background fabric square and draw around it with your temporary fabric marker pen. This will help you position your applique shapes.
- Trace the reindeer shapes and antlers onto the paper side of your Bondaweb, cut out roughly, then iron onto the reverse of your fabric. Allow a little extra at the ends of the antlers and the bottom of the back reindeer to underlap the other shapes. Cut out shapes using long smooth cuts to avoid jagged edges. Using illustration as a guide position applique pieces - the reindeer body should end ½ to ¾" below the bottom edge of the square you drew and the edge of the front deer is ¾ " from the left-hand edge of the square.

- When you're happy with the positioning of your reindeer, press with a hot iron (using a cloth to protect your felt/fabric if necessary) to fuse into position. Secure shapes around edges with small straight stitches worked at right angles to the edges in two strands of matching floss.

- Stitch eyes in black floss and noses in black and red floss. Add a tiny white stitch to each eye for sparkle.

- Stitch buttons to antlers using red and green floss randomly. Add strings in gold floss. Stitch pink buttons for cheeks and cream buttons for markings - or alternatively use satin stitch and two strands of pink and cream floss to indicate these.

- Cut out letter shapes in the same way as your reindeer shapes. You may find embroidery scissors useful for cutting out the centres of the "R"s and "A". Fuse each letter to a scrap of brightly coloured felt, then cut a square or rectangle around the letter with your pinking shears if you have them. The squares/rectangles don't have to be exactly the same size - in fact it's better if they aren't.

- Position your letters and squares on your panel, using the photograph as a guide and securing in place with temporary fabric adhesive spray.

- Fit the embroidery foot to your sewing machine and drop the feed dogs. With gold thread in your needle machine around the edges of each letter twice. This will hold both the letter and the felt square in place, there's no need to stitch the felt square separately to the fabric.

- Press your work lightly from the back, taking care not to damage the buttons.

Mount piece and add lights:

- Position your work centrally on the canvas block, fold excess fabric to the back and secure in place with your staple gun. Work from the centre of each side outwards (do top and bottom first, then the two sides), ensuring your fabric is taut but not too tight as this might distort your work. Mitre the corners, trimming away excess fabric.

- With your hot glue gun, glue your ribbon all around the edge of the board.

- With your temporary fabric marker pen, mark dots where you want your lights to go - see the diagram at the top of this page.

- Push the points of your embroidery scissors through the board and fabric from the front backwards, and then back to front, wiggling them a little to make sure the hole is big enough to take your light.

- Push each bulb through the hole, making sure it goes right through and the bulb is clear of the fabric. Work in a logical sequence around your picture so that the wire between each bulb isn't stretched.

- Use a blob of glue at the back of each bulb to hold them in place. The battery unit will sit on the bottom of the wooden frame - I didn't need to glue mine n place which will make it much easier to change the batteries.

Make sure your bulbs are pushed right through and are clear of the fabric. Only use cool-touch LED battery operated lights.

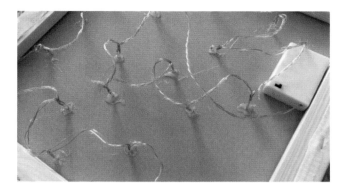

The back of the canvas block. The lights are held n place with a blob of glue and the battery unit sits on the base of the frame.

- Remove any visible lines left by your temporary fabric marker. Your picture is now finished.

15

Christmas Cards and Crackers

Sending and receiving cards is still an important part of Christmas, even in the age of the email, whilst we all love the silly jokes and paper hats found inside our Christmas crackers. But have you ever paused to wonder how these traditions began?

Two of the most popular latecomers to our Christmas festivities came about as a direct result of Victorian enterprise and technology in the 19th century. Christmas crackers were invented by a one man – a man with a great idea; whilst Christmas cards were the outcome of a series of improvements in printing techniques together with the introduction of the penny post.

The first Christmas card

Controversy surrounds the date of the first Christmas card and the name of its creator, although the credit is generally given to Sir Henry Cole, the first director of the Victoria and Albert Museum, and artist John Calcott Horsley RA. In 1843 Horsley designed a card following the suggestion of his friend Cole and in 1846 a thousand copies were sold at a shilling each by a printing company in Old Bond Street, London. The image on the card is of a family merrily drinking wine and the two side panels show charitable activities. It bore the greeting "A Merry Christmas and Happy New Year to You."

Christmas cards didn't become generally popular until the development of cheaper printing techniques (a shilling was a lot of money back in 1843 - round about £40 in today's money) and the introduction of a halfpenny stamp for cards in 1870, but they then quickly became so popular that by 1880 the Post Office was asking everyone to post their cards early to be sure they'd reach the intended recipients in time for Christmas - sounds familiar!!

Early Christmas card designs were more Dickensian than religious and often featured stagecoaches and snowy landscapes, Christmas puddings and Yule logs and the ever popular robin redbreast. Indeed, the idea of the robin as a Christmas bird was reinforced as the early postmen delivering these cards were also known as Robins due to the colour of their uniform.

A Victorian card

Over the following decades, cards became more and more exotic, featuring silk fringes, gilding and satin and plush insets. They appeared in the shape of fans, stars, scrolls and other novelty cutouts.

The first Christmas cards reached America in the 1850s, but only became popular with the work of Louis Prang, a printer of German origin living in Roxbury, Massachusetts, who printed his first cards in 1875. They were extremely high quality and at first featured mainly floral designs, though later he printed more seasonal designs such as the Madonna and Child and Santa Claus. He helped to popularise Christmas cards by organising nationwide competitions for the best designs. But sadly Prang was unable to comete witht he influx of cheaper cards from Europe in the 18090s and eventually gave up that side of his business.

Early Louis Prang Card

Unlike Christmas cards where there's more than one contender for the title of "the first" there's no dispute about the inventor of the Christmas cracker. Tom Smith was a confectioner's apprentice before setting up his own business making wedding cake decorations. In 1847, whilst visiting Paris, France in search of new ideas, he spotted sugared almonds wrapped in twists of coloured tissue paper in a shop window. He hurried home and introduced the British public to these delightful "bon-bons" which proved to be quite popular. However demand dropped sharply after Christmas, so Smith decided to concentrate on the seasonal angle. First love messages, then toys, charms, jokes and jewellery joined the almond inside the wrapping - but still something was missing.

Then, one winter's evening whilst Tom Smith was sitting at home listening to the comforting crackle of his log fire a sensational idea struck him - he would put a bang into his bon-bons. In 1860, following two years of experimentation, he hit upon the saltpetre friction strip. Crackers - as his bon-bons were now known - became immensely popular, and over the years all kinds of novelties went into the cardboard cracker tube. Arctic expeditions were commemorated with miniature bears and bear masks, there were mottoes for cricketers, crackers for bachelors and trinkets and jokes of all kinds. But the most consistent theme was love, with sentimental trinkets, verses and mottoes for all.

Wish Upon a Star: Mr Fox

Cute little fox wishing upon a star for his dreams to come true. From a drawing by Flapdoodledesigns, the finished embroidery is shown mounted in a 7" hoop.

Pattern includes link to video tutorial on stitching Mr Fox's fur - it's easy when you know how!

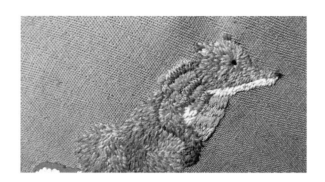

You will need:

- 8" square medium weight non-stretchy cotton, linen or cotton/linen blend fabric. Quilting weight fabric will be too light for this piece of work as you're going to be doing a lot of dense stitching!

- DMC stranded cotton floss in colours 310, 321, 435, 498, 677, 807, 906, 918, 920, 945, 3021, 3826, 3864, E168, blanc, ecru

Bustle & Sew

Love to Sew and Sew with Love...

"How to Stitch Fur"

featuring Mr Fox

"Wish upon a Star"

www.bustleandsew.com

Please CLICK HERE to access video with full step by step instructions for stitching Mr Fox or type the following url into your browser address bar:

http://bustleandsew.com/mr-fox-how-to-stitch-fur/

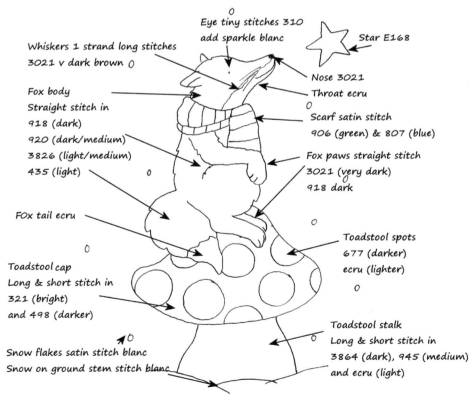

Eye tiny stitches 310
add sparkle blanc

Star E168

Whiskers 1 strand long stitches
3021 v dark brown

Nose 3021

Throat ecru

Fox body
Straight stitch in
918 (dark)
920 (dark/medium)
3826 (light/medium)
435 (light)

Scarf satin stitch
906 (green) & 807 (blue)

Fox paws straight stitch
3021 (very dark)
918 dark

FOx tail ecru

Toadstool spots
677 (darker)
ecru (lighter)

Toadstool cap
Long & short stitch in
321 (bright)
and 498 (darker)

Toadstool stalk
Long & short stitch in
3864 (dark), 945 (medium)
and ecru (light)

Snow flakes satin stitch blanc
Snow on ground stem stitch blanc

Feed the birds this winter ....

As truly wild habitats for birds become fewer and farms provide fewer opportunities for foraging, our gardens are becoming increasingly important for the survival of many species of bird.

Centuries ago many birds would have lived through the winter months on the rich pickings found around farms and in the fields when men and machinery were not as efficient as they are today, and plenty of nourishment was to be found lying in rick-yards and at field edges months after the harvest had been gathered in. Today crops are gathered quickly and precisely and stored away into vast secure silos that offer no access to wildlife. Species that once sheltered and lived along hedgerows are increasingly moving into our towns and villages and gardens where they rely upon humans for providing much of their food - whether intentionally or not.

When we plant fruit trees and plants that produce berries and seeds we are providing the means of survival through the harshest months of the year to many species of birds and animals.

Small birds are generally seen as beneficial visitors to our gardens - and I know I love to watch the antics of my winter visitors. As a child I remember hanging up scraps of fat and coconut halves for the birds with my mum and now we are likely to provide peanuts, seeds or special bird cakes too. I don't throw out scraps such as bread crusts as these are likely to attract both hungry Newfoundland dogs and vermin such as rats. It's much better to hang things that will keep the birds busy and that will feed the most number of species.

Fruit left to ripen then drop from trees or vines gives rich pickings to many birds at the beginning of the winter, whilst some crab apples and dessert apples are very late to mature, so are excellent for birds when the weather grows colder and food is harder to find.

Goldfinch on thistle

Try not to be too tidy in the garden, leave thistle-type plants to flower and resist cutting the dead blooms so that finches and other seed-eaters will be able to enjoy them. Cotoneaster and pyracantha will hold their berries for weeks, and are often visited by birds in England in late winter once more perishable fruits have all disappeared. Many small birds rely on over-wintering grubs and insects in tree bark so avoid pesticides and don't be too quick to clear away old or dead branches.

It's fun to make special food for the birds that visit your garden - I remember when Rosie was a little girl we often used to make bird cakes for them to enjoy - and at Christmas time decorate them with sprigs of holly and hang with red twine so the birds could enjoy their Christmas dinner too.

Bird Cakes

This recipe can be adapted in a limitless number of ways depending upon what ingredients you have to hand, or can acquire, and what will be suitable for the kinds of birds you'll be feeding.

Fat is a most important part of the cake as it is the binder for all the other ingredients as well as providing plenty of instant energy in cold weather for birds who need to eat huge quantities of food - sometimes multiples of their own bodyweight - to keep them alive when the daylight foraging hours are short and the nights are long and cold. You can add grated suet with the dry ingredients too if you want. Either mould your cakes in discs to fit a wire feeder or make round balls to wrap in wire mesh and hang from a garden tree or bird table.

You will need:

- approx 8 oz (225 g) solid white vegetable fat
- 1 cup oatmeal
- 1 cup chopped nuts
- 1 cup flaked maize
- 1 cup kibbled wheat
- 1 cup mixed wild bird seed
- 1 cup vine fruits, chopped **or**
- 6 cups ready-made wild bird seed mixture.

Gently melt the fat in a large pan. Put the dry ingredients into a large bowl and pour the fat over them. Stir the mixture until the fat is really well mixed with the dry ingredients. The amount of fat you'll need is dependent upon the dry ingredients you've used, so add sufficient to obtain a mixture that holds together as the fat begins to cool. With damp hands pat the mixture into small cakes or balls or pour into shallow moulds. Leave in a cold place to set firm.

Another Flapdoodledesign!

Marching Elephants Applique

This is a really easy, but amazingly effective design to make for a child's room, or simply for yourself if you love cheerful colours! The pattern is taken from a mid-century colouring book - it's simple machine embroidery, with a few hand-stitched details. I have created my elephants on a 12" square panel, but you can resize the pattern to whatever size you want ... a cushion would look great - or why not trim some bedding or

You will need:

- 15" square panel of backing fabric - any fabric will do as long as it is smooth and not stretchy. The actual design measures about 12" square, but if you're planning to mount your design, or make a cover from it, then you'll need a little extra for borders.
- 4 x 8" squares felt for elephants in greys, beiges or other suitable colours
- Scraps of fabric for head-dresses and saddle cloths
- 4 buttons for head-dresses
- Black and a lighter colour thread suitable for your sewing machine. Black for the needle and a lighter colour in the bobbin.
- Small amount black embroidery floss
- Small amount brightly-coloured embroidery floss
- Bondaweb
- 12" square artist's canvas block
- Staple gun
- Temporary fabric marker pen
- Embroidery foot for your sewing machine

Directions:

- Place your fabric right side up on a clean flat surface. Place your canvas block in the centre of the fabric and draw around it with the temporary fabric marker pen. This will help you position your elephants.

- Using the templates (actual size) trace two left-facing and two right-facing elephants on to the paper side of your Bondaweb. Cut out roughly and fuse to the felt, then cut out your elephants. Make long smooth cuts to avoid jagged edges.

- Fold your fabric in 4 and, using the creases as a guide, position your elephants. When you're happy with their positioning, fuse into place, protecting the felt with a cloth.

- Cut, position and fuse head-dresses and saddle-cloths in the same way.

- Drop the feed dogs on your sewing machine. Using black thread at the top and grey or another dark coloured thread in the bobbin, stitch around the edges of each elephant and the head-dresses, saddle-cloths. (Note: using light thread in the bobbin gives a less solid line - using black in both makes your line too solid and heavy)

- Now stitch around again, but this time stitch the tummies, knees and toenails using the picture as a guide. Remember that with this kind of applique your stitching doesn't have to be too neat. In fact, it's nicer if it isn't (up to a limit of course).

- Using the marker pen, mark in position of eyes and ears. Stitch ears using two lines of machining as before, and work eyes as French knots (2 strands of floss and two twists). If you don't like working French knots, then you could always work two small satin stitches instead. Work stars on saddle-cloths.

- Press your work on the reverse, then secure buttons in place using bright coloured floss.

- Mount your work on the canvas block. Align the line you drew with the top edge of the block, turn the fabric to the back and working from the centre outwards staple into place with your staple gun. Repeat along the bottom edge making sure the fabric is taut but not tight. Staple the sides in the same way, mitring the corners and trimming away excess fabric.

- FINISHED!!

Handstitched Christmas

A Collection of Seasonal Designs

Christmas is a wonderful time of year when you welcome friends and family into your home. Handmade decorations add extra seasonal sparkle and you're sure to discover plenty of inspiration inside this little book.

Choose from Angel Pigs, Sleepy Baby Owls, Reindeer and of course the Nativity - or why not make them all?

Helen Dickson

The First Christmas Tree

(traditional story)

Once upon a time, in a forest far away grew a great many pine trees. Most of them were tall trees, higher than the houses that we see, and with wide, strong branches. But there was one tree that was not nearly so tall as the others; in fact, it was no taller than some of the children in the kindergarten.

Now, the tall trees could see far, far out over the hilltops and into the valleys, and they could hear all the noises that went on in the world beyond the forest, but Little Tree was so small and the other trees grew so high and thick about it that it could not see nor hear these things at all; but the other trees were very kind, and they would stoop down and tell them to Little Tree. One night in the winter time there seemed to be something strange happening in the little town among the hills, for the trees did not go to sleep after the sun went down, but put their heads together and spoke in strange, low whispers that were full of awe and wonder. The Little Tree, from its place close down to the ground, did not understand what it was all about. It listened awhile, and then lifted its head as high as ever it could and shouted to its tall neighbour:

"Please tell me what is happening?"

And the big tree leaned down and whispered:

"The shepherds out on the hilltops are telling strange stories while they watch their sheep. The air is filled with sweet music, and there is a wonderful star coming up in the east, travelling westward always, and the shepherds say that they are waiting for it to stop and shine over a humble stable in their little town. I don't know why it is going to stop there, but I will look again and listen."

So the tall tree lifted up its head again, and reached far out so that it might hear more of the wonderful story. Bye and bye it leant down again, and whispered to the Little Tree:

"Oh, Little Tree, listen! There are angels among the shepherds on the hills, and they are all talking together. They seem to be awaiting the birth of a little child, who will be a king among the people, and the beautiful star will shine above the stable where the little king will be laid in a manger."

The tall tree again raised its head to listen, and Little Tree, much puzzled, thought within itself: "It is very strange, indeed, oooh, how I wish that I could see it all!"

The Little Tree waited a little longer until everything grew quiet, and a great peace came upon the forest. Then suddenly the town, and even the forest was illuminated with a strange, white light that made everything as bright as day, and the air was filled with the flutter of angels' wings, and with music such as the world had never heard before. The people and the trees, and even the stars in the heaven, lifted up their voices and sang together while the whole world was filled with music and joy and love for the little Christ-child who had come to dwell upon the earth.

Little Tree was full of fear and wonder, for so great was the excitement that all the other trees had almost forgotten it, and it could not understand the mysterious sounds; but before too long its tall friend leaned down again and said:
"Listen, listen, Little Tree! Such news I have to tell! The Christ has come—the King! And the whole world is singing such beautiful music. There are wise men coming from the East, bringing beautiful gifts to the Christ-child. The angels, too, have come down to the earth, and they bear gifts of gold and rare, beautiful stones. Wait! I will tell you more."

The tall tree had scarcely lifted up its head when it leaned down again and whispered to Little Tree:

"Look! Look! Little Tree! They are coming this way; the angels are coming here, into our forest! Lift up your head high and you will see them as they pass."

Then Little Tree lifted up its head and saw the white flutter of angel robes and heard the beautiful, sweet voices of the heavenly host who came with precious gifts into the forest.

Transfers in the Templates Section

"Oh," said Little Tree, "they are coming here, toward me! What shall I do?" And in fear it bent its head so low that it almost touched the ground. But the music came nearer and nearer, and the Little Tree felt a tender hand upon its branches, and a soft, gentle voice said to it:

"Arise, Little Tree, and come with us, for we have come into the forest to seek you. Yes, you, the very smallest among the trees, are to be our gift-bearer. Come; lift up your head."

In fear and trembling Little Tree did as the angel bade it. But when it looked into the angel's face and saw the love and kindness there, all fear was gone, and it said to the angel:

"Yes; make me ready. I will come with you to the little Christ-child in the manger."

So all the angels brought their gifts of precious jewels and shining gold, and fastened them upon the branches of the Little Tree. Then the leader of the angels' band took up the Little Tree from the ground and bore it, laden with its precious burden, to the feet of the Christ-child, the first Christmas Tree of all.

Holly & Berry

Inspired by vintage design - and brought right up to date for this Christmas - meet Holly and Berry, the baby reindeer. They measure just 10 ½" tall and will make a perfect addition to your decorations this Christmas.

Holly and Berry have wired legs, button noses and black beads for eyes so are not suitable for toys - they are decorative only.

return and complete the cross stitch in the other direction. This gives a strong, but also decorative, stitch.

- Seam allowances are included.

- Use two strands of floss throughout.

Method:

- Cut out all pieces as indicated on the templates (actual size).

- Sew on the white face markings. Place them in position on the head (see template for guidance) and then stitch around curved edge with short straight stitches worked at right angles to the edge of the face marking. Trim away the surplus main body felt beneath the white face markings so that you have only one thickness of felt at the seams (if you don't do this then the main body felt will show through at the seams and make a line down the middle of the reindeer's nose and chin)

- Make ears and tail by placing a coloured and cream piece together and stitching all the way round in the same way as the body. Then fold in half lengthways with the cream felt inside and stitch together at the base. Remember to make the two ears the opposite way round to each other to form a pair. It doesn't matter which way round you stitch the tail.

- Stitch body gussets to main body as shown by red dotted lines in the diagram on the next page. Join body gussets along the centre line from C to D.

- Prepare your leg wires. Bend ½" up at each end of the wires to form a narrow loop and bind with fabric sticking plaster. The 11 ½" piece is for the front legs and the 12" piece for the back legs. Bend each wire in half and then bend to the contour of the legs. Slip in from the top of the body. Sew up the bottom ½" of the leg, then insert some stuffing. Continue stitching up the legs, inserting stuffing as you go and ensuring that the wire is embedded in the stuffing. Stuff firmly - your stuffing stick will be invaluable here. Only use very small pieces of stuffing at

You will need:

- 9" x 18" piece (or two 9" squares) of felt for the main body

- 9" square cream felt

- Scraps of black felt

- Stranded cotton floss or perle thread for seams (choose a colour that either matches or contrasts with your main body colour - I used brown for Berry and ecru for Holly)

- Pink stranded cotton floss for cheeks

- ½" button for nose

- Toy stuffing

- 2 lengths of 2 mm wire, one piece 11 ½" long and the other 12" long

- Fabric sticking plaster tape

- Toy stuffing

- Stuffing stick - this can be a simple bamboo skewer - break the pointed tip off and then fray the end so it can "grab" the stuffing - essential for stuffing narrow places.

Notes:

- All pieces are joined with wrong sides together. Work half cross stitch in one direction, then

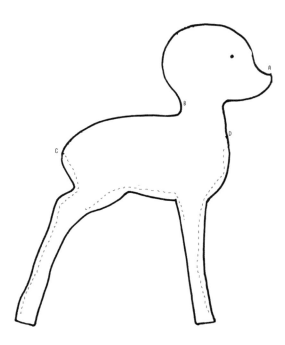

- Add hooves - oversew the upper part around each leg, making a seam at the back. Stitch a sole to each hoof and push in a little stuffing before you close the seam to make sure the base of each leg is quite firm and the loop at the end of the wire is well covered.

- Bend the legs into a nice position so that your baby reindeer stands firmly without wobbling.

- Add the eyes - mark their position first with glass-headed pins - just a fraction of an inch difference will really affect your reindeer's expression so you need to get this right! When you're happy with their position stitch the black beads to the sides of the head, taking a few stitches through the head from eye to eye and pulling to slightly sink the eyes into the head.

- Stitch the button to the end of the nose and make a few straight stitches in pink floss for the cheeks.

- Cut out 8 or 10 small circles of cream felt and stitch to rump for markings.

- Your reindeer is now finished!

at a time as you don't want your legs to be lumpy. Your wire should be so well covered in stuffing that you can't feel it. Repeat for all four legs

- Join at head from D to A, then insert head gusset between A and B, inserting folded ears as indcated on the template. Stitch along one side from A to B first, then a little away along the other side inserting stuffing as you go to make sure the nose is nice and firm. The actual neck is quite narrow and it will be hard to push too much stuffing up through the gap, so be sure to mostly stuff the head before you finish seaming the gusset at B. You can add more small pieces to make the head nice and firm at this point, and also stuff around the front of the chest, again making sure the wire is well covered by the stuffing.

- Stitch along back from C to B, inserting folded tail on the curve of the rump. Again stuff as you go, making sure the body is nice and firm before you close the seam completely. Use your stuffing stick to make sure the legs are well filled where they join the body.

Traditional Parlour Games

Christmas is the time to put away the X-box or PlayStation and enjoy some traditional family fun - and if you're stuck for ideas here's a few traditional favourites to choose from ...

None of these games require any specialist or expensive equipment or supplies - most of what you'll need I'm sure you'll already have in the house …

Hunt the Ring

Thread a ring or key onto a long piece of string which is then knotted to form a circle. The company stands in a circle holding the string and slides the ring or key rapidly from hand to hand. One member of the party stands in the centre of the circle and has to guess who holds the ring at any given time. If s/he guesses right then the holder becomes the hunter.

The Minister's Cat

This is probably the best known of many alphabetical games.

The first player might say "The minister's cat is an angry cat;" then the other players n turn repeat the sentence each using a different

adjective to describe the cat beginning with the letter "A". They then move onto "B" and so on through the alphabet. Players who cannot think of an adjective beginning with the right letter, or who repeat one already used, drop out until only the winner remains.

Elements

One member of the company throws a soft ball to another, at the same time naming one of the elements - earth, air, water or fire. If one of the first three elements is given, the person catching the ball has to name an animal living in the element within a count of ten. For example, if water is called, the catcher might say, "Whale." Anyone speaking when "fire" is called, or naming an animal wrongly, pays a forfeit. The catcher then throws the ball to another member of the group.

Cheat

Deal a pack of cards to any number of players. They look at their cards, then the player on the left of the dealer opens by laying his lowest card (ace is lowest) face down on the table and calling out what it is. The next player puts his card face downwards and calls the next number. For example, if the first player played two, then the second must call three. The players don't have to put down the card with the number they call and any other player may challenge them by calling "Cheat!" If that happens the player must turn up his card and if it isn't the same as the number he called he must pick up all the cards on the table. If it is then the challenger collects the cards. The first player to get rid of all their card wins.

Some Puzzles

Six Rows Puzzle

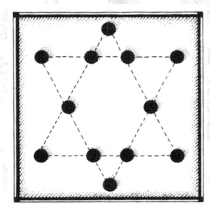

Place twelve counters in six rows so that there are four counters in each row - answer above.

Two Squares

How do you draw the image below without ever removing your pencil from the paper - without crossing any line or retracing any part?

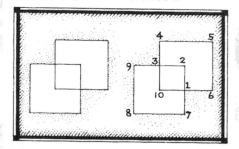

Answer: Draw a line in the following sequence: 1 to 2 to 3 to 4 to 5 to 6 to 1 to 7 to 8 to 9 to 3 to 10 to 1

Make a 9

How can you add five lines to the six matches shown below and make nine?

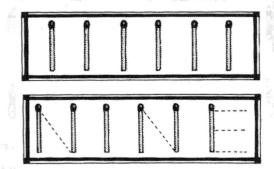

Answer: draw in the lines as shown in the diagram above.

And finally ... my most favourite (and terrible) Christmas joke ever .....

"What's Santa's favourite sort of pizza?"

"Deep pan, crisp and even!"

Merry Christmas everyone xx

Santa Christmas Apron

If your Christmas jumper's too woolly and you're beginning to feel as roasted as the Christmas turkey - then help is at hand! Keep the festive feel with this Santa apron featuring an easy machine applique Santa - but wear as much (or as little!) underneath as you like! Comfort guaranteed!

- Bondaweb

- Temporary fabric marker pen

- Black and light coloured thread for your sewing machine for the applique, and a colour to match your background fabric to make up the apron.

- Invisible thread for attaching the ric-rac braid

- 1" button

Apron:

This design will work well on a "normal" apron - if you have one you particularly like, then use that as a template to cut your fabric. In this case you will need tape for your apron strings. I have a different pattern that I use - no strings, but a more wrap-round style fastened at the back with a single button. Here's the pattern with measurements - you'll need to draw it out on newspaper or tracing pa

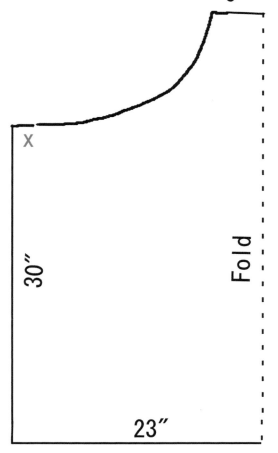

You will need:

- 48" wide x 48" long piece of medium weight cotton fabric

- 12" square cream wool blend felt

- 8" x 6" red wool blend felt

- 6" x 4" flesh colour wool blend felt

- Scraps of wool blend felt in black, green , white and yellow

- White and black stranded cotton embroidery floss

- 60" red ric-rac braid (optional)

- 1" button

Cut out your apron front first. Then position your applique centrally and about 6" down from the top edge.

Applique:

- The template is given full sized - you will need to join the two pieces - this should be easy as it's obvious how they overlap. It's also reversed ready for you to trace onto the paper side of your Bondaweb.

- Trace all the shapes onto your Bondaweb, cut out roughly, then fuse to the appropriate coloured felt and cut out.

- Position shapes on your apron front, in the centre and with the top of Santa's hat about 6" from the top edge. Work from the bottom upwards - so start with the beard, then face, hat, hat trim, mouth and moustache - then add holly leaves, eyebrows and bell. The eyes are white and blue felt - don't use the cream as you want his eyes to be bright and sparkly.

- When you're happy with the positioning of your shapes fuse into place with a hot iron (protect the felt with a cloth), then turn your work over and fuse again from the back.

- Fit the embroidery foot to your sewing machine and drop your feed dogs. With black thread in your needle and light coloured in your bobbin (for a less "solid" line) stitch around the edges of the shapes - see the picture on previous page for guidance.

- Draw in lines with your temporary fabric marker pen for nose and on beard and machine stitch.

- Add the pupils in black floss and tiny white stitches for the sparkles.

- With your temporary fabric marker pen draw in the shiny reflections on Santa's face and stitch in satin stitch in white floss.

- Press your work well from the back.

Make up your Apron:

- From your main fabric cut a rectangle measuring 25 ½" x 2" and 7 ½" squares

- With right sides together fold the long rectangle lengthways down the centre and stitch the long side 1/4" from the edge. Turn right side out and press seam to the centre of the back.

- Turn the curved edges of the main piece under ¼" and then ½" and press. Unfold and clip the edge as far as the ¼" fold to help it lie flat. Refold and press again, then machine stitch and press.

- Align the short edges of the neck rectangle with the top corners of your main piece, pin into place, then turn both the neck and main piece under ¼" and then ½". Press and machine stitch.

- With invisible thread in your needle machine stitch red ric-rac braid along bottom of apron, 2" up from bottom edge.

- Hem sides and bottom of apron - turn under ½ and then 1", press and machine stitch.

- With invisible thread in your needle machine stitch red ric-rac braid along tops of 7" squares, 1 ¾" down from the top. Turn top under ¼" an then ½" and top stitch. Turn sides of square under ½". Position patch pockets in the most comfortable place for you - try apron on before decding - then pin and topstitch to main part of apron.

- Stitch button to one side of apron back (position marked by red X on template) and make buttonhole on the other side.

- Your apron is now finished.

These children have been so good all the year.
I really must leave some nice presents here.

Nativity Set

Colourful collection of Nativity figures guaranteed to brighten up your home this Christmas! As well as Mary, Joseph, baby Jesus and the Shepherds, this month brings the Three Kings who have travelled from the corners of the globe - Africa, the Arctic and Europe - and there's even a camel!

Figures stand approximately 4" tall.

The three figures are all made using the same templates and differ only in their decoration. I'll give you the instructions for making the basic cone-shaped figure first, then the details for each one.

To make one basic figure you will need:

- 6" square of body/base fabric

- 2" x 1" piece of sleeve fabric

- 4" x 6" flesh coloured felt for face & hands

- 2" square cardboard

- Strong thread

- Small beach pebble/polybeads or rice to weight base (optional)

- Toy stuffing

- Temporary fabric marker pen

- Stranded cotton embroidery floss in black and pink for features and matching your body fabric for attaching base and head fabric for joining head.

Method for basic figure:

- Cut out all pieces from template

- Decorate cone shaped body piece as per instructions for figure you are making.

- Fold the cone shape in half, right sides together and machine stitch down straight edge with a ¼" or less seam allowance. Turn right side out and stuff from the neck end down to just before the base.

- With wrong sides together join base to body using cross stitch or blanket stitch. Insert cardboard circle and stuffing wrapped pebble if using before closing seam. Insert more stuffing from head end if necessary to make body firm.

- With your strong thread run a gathering thread around the edge of your flesh-coloured felt circle. Insert a small amount of stuffing and draw up

thread fairly tightly. Knot and then lace across back of head to create an oval-shape for the face.

- With matching floss stitch flesh-coloured oval to back of head to hide the lacing and attach head to top of body.

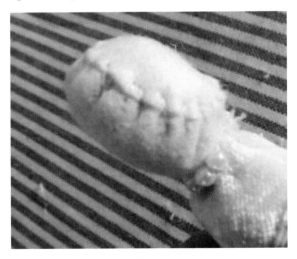

- With your temporary fabric marker pen draw features onto front of face. These are very simple - just follow the photos as a guide. Stitch the features in a single strand of black floss and back stitch - the eyes are tiny stitches placed very closely together. Then add pink cheeks - just a couple of straight stitches in pink floss.

- Your basic figure is now completed.

Mary:

In addition to the materials for the basic figure you will need:

- 6" x 4" rectangle white fabric for headdress/collar

- Bright blue, gold and brown stranded cotton floss

- 2 x ¼" mother of pearl buttons

- Pinking shears (optional)

- Cut collar from template - applique to top of body shape with small straight stitches at right-angles to edge of fabric. Add some small French knots with 2 strands of floss.

- Cut and applique arms and hands in the same way, overlapping the ends of the hands with the sleeves

- Work feather stitch around base of figure, ½" up from the edge using 3 strands of floss

- Stitch buttons to front of dress.

- Now make up figure as instructions for basic figure.

- Add hair to front of head using 2 strands of floss and bullion stitch (there is no need to work at back as it won't be seen). If you're unfamiliar with bullion stitch then you'll find instructions for working in my free e-book "Simple Stitchery".

- Cut headdress using pinking shears if you have them for a nice decorative touch. Fold in half lengthways to find centre of headdress, then pin to head, making sure that it's centred - ie both sides are the same length. Stitch to head with matching thread and tiny stitches, and also stitch at neck and arms, shaping the headdress around Mary's body.

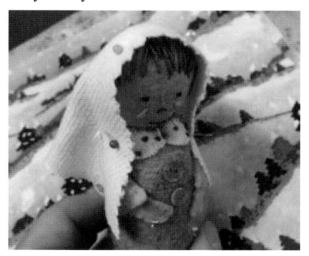

- Cut a length of gold floss sufficient to go around Mary's head, and a few extra inches to work with. Bring up through headdress at back of head, and take down in the same place, couching the circle of floss into place on the head with small stitches in cream thread.

- Mary is now finished.

- Add hair using bullion stitch and work features as for Mary

- Cut beard shape and stitch to front of face, adding extra stitches above mouth.

- Add headdress as Mary, but instead of gold metallic floss use string for headdress.

- Joseph is now finished.

Joseph:

In addition to the materials for the basic figure you will need:

- 6" x 4" rectangle of fabric for headdress

- Scrap of brown felt for beard

- Brown (to match beard felt), black, pink embroidery floss

- 6" x 4" rectangle of brown fabric for cloak

- Piece of string for headdress

- Pinking shears (optional)

- Applique hands and sleeves into place, then make up body as for basic figure

- Cut cloak shape and applique to body, centering over back seam.

Angel:

In addition to the materials for the basic figure you will need:

- 3" x 4" rectangle of fabric for headdress

- Yellow knitting yarn

- 16 small pearl beads

- 2 x 5" square fabric for wings

- 5" square cardboard for wings

- Thin tinsel

- Gold embroidery floss

- 6" x 5" pretty fabric for robe overlay

- Pinking shears (optional)

- Cut a second body piece 1¼ " shorter along the curved edge and stitch into place on top of man body piece. If you have them it's nice to use pinking shears to cut the curved edge

- Applique hands and arms as before using small straight stitches at right angles to edge of fabric. Add border of cross stitch in gold floss alternate with pearl beads to the bottom of the robe ½ " up from the bottom edge (see below) and add running stitch to the bottom of the robe overlay

- Make up as for basic figure

- Work loopy stitches in knitting yarn all over the front and sides of the head. Take small back stitches between the loops to hold the yarn securely. When covered trim to about ½" in length and fluff the ends of the yarn.

-

- Thread beads onto length of thread and give your angel a pearl necklace.

- Add headdress as before though this time it's a shorter length so you don't need to stitch to neck and shoulders.

- Cut wings from template and join back to front with cross stitch or blanket stitch. Insert cardboard stiffening when you're part way round.

- Stitch wings to top back of angel and bend until you achieve desired position.

- Your angel is now finished.

Jesus

- For the baby Jesus cut a rectangle of white felt measuring 2 ½" x 2"

- With right sides together fold in half, then machine stitch along one short and the long side. Turn right side out and stuff lightly. Run a gathering thread along the other short edge and pull up tightly.

- Add small oval for face, eyes are tiny black stitches and pink for cheeks. Hair is bullion stitch as before

- Run a spiral of back stitch around body to represent swathing bands.

Manger:

- Cut a rectangle of brown fabric measuring 4" x 2 ½" and pinch up ½" at the corners. Stitch corners into place.

- Cut two rectangles of straw coloured felt measuring 4 ½"x 3" - choose one light and one darker colour. Cut into the edges for about ¾" as shown (need not be exact) and cut a ¾ " square from the corners to reduce bulk (see above).

- Push in the first straw rectangle, then add a little stuffing.

- Cover stuffing with second straw rectangle and push down to make a nice nest shape, securing with a few stitches.

- Your manger is now finished.

Shepherd & Sheep:

In addition to the materials for the basic figure you will need:

- 6" x 4" rectangle stripey fabric for headdress

- 6" x 4" rectangle brown fabric for cloak

- 2 pieces fleece fabric measuring 1 ¼" x 1 ½" each

- 2 tiny scraps black felt for sheeps' heads

- Piece of string for headdress

- Brown stranded cotton floss

- Pinking shears (optional)

Make your figure:

- Applique cloak and hand to front of body shape. Make the cloak on the left ½" longer than the body shape, so there will be room to tuck in the little sheep.

- To make the sheep roll each piece of fleece into a sausage shape with the fleece on the outside and stitch with cream thread.

- Fold the head shape in half and stitch to the front of the sheep.

- Stitch one sheep to the side of the figure - partly cover with cloak and then stitch cloak down side and at bottom.

- Stitch the other sheep to the other side of the figure, as though it's standing next to the shepherd.

- Applique hand and arm in place as shown.

- Now make up figure as instructions for basic figure.

- Add hair to front of head using 2 strands of floss and bullion stitch (there is no need to work at back as it won't be seen). If you're unfamiliar with bullion stitch then you'll find instructions for working in my free e-book "Simple Stitchery".

- Cut headdress using pinking shears if you have them for a nice decorative touch. Fold in half

lengthways to find centre of headdress, then pin to head, making sure that it's centred - ie both sides are the same length. Stitch to head with matching thread and tiny stitches, and also stitch at neck and arms, shaping the headdress around the shepherd's body.

- Cut a length of string sufficient to go around head, and a few extra inches to work with. Bring up through headdress at back of head, and take down in the same place, couching the circle of floss into place on the head with small stitches.

The Three Kings

These also use the basic template and although I'll give you the material requirements for each of my kings, this really is a great opportunity for you to dig deep in your boxes of scraps, remnants and buttons to create your own kings …

Scandinavian King

Innuit King

- His body is trimmed with scraps of coloured fabric and I stitched running stitch around the base of his body with 6 strands of gold floss before makng up the figure.

- The gift is three wooden beads joined with gold floss and stitched to his body.

- His hair is actually some sheep's wool I collected off a wire fence when out on a walk with Daisy and Ben, but wool roving would work just as well. It's secured to his head with tiny stitches in cream thread.

- His crown is simply a circle of ricrac braid with a shiny gold button at the front.

- He is probably the easiest king - with no hands, arms or even hair!

- He is wrapped in a trimming of real fur - I purchased a bag of scraps from a reputable English footwear company, the leftovers from their sheepskin boots so I am fine with their provenance. If you don't want to use real fur, then fake fur is fine and probably easier to use. If using real fur then it's easiest to glue the hide in place as it can be hard to stitch. His hat is simply another small piece of fur wrapped around his head.

- The scarf is a ¾" x 4" piece of felted wool fabric simply knotted around his neck

- His present is a button and a couple of beads stitched to his body.

- Notice his cheeks are rosy red with the cold rather than pink.

African King

Camel

- Fun and funky chenille hair, simply stitched as long loopy stitches to the back of his head - I used a multi-coloured yarn for even more fun!

- He wears a crown of ¼" buttons stitched to his head and also a necklace the same.

- The gift is two large buttons stitched to his body which was also trimmed with red ricrac braid before making up.

- This is a really easy make - just cut out two bodies and two gussets from camel-coloured felt - you'll need a 12" square of felt.

- Stitch gussets to main body pieces around legs, then stitch all around camel using a machine zig-zag stitch. Stuff and then close the centre gusset seam by hand. Stitch ears into place and add eyes with black floss.

- His bridle is just the same chenille yarn as the king's hair wrapped around his head and his saddle just rectangles of felt topped with a 1" button stitched to his body.

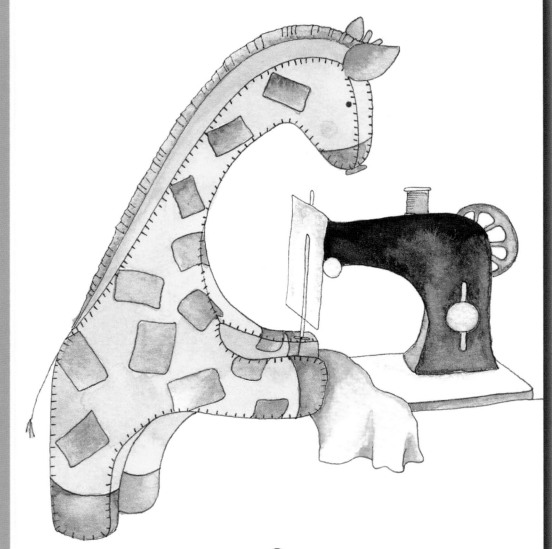

Pattern Templates

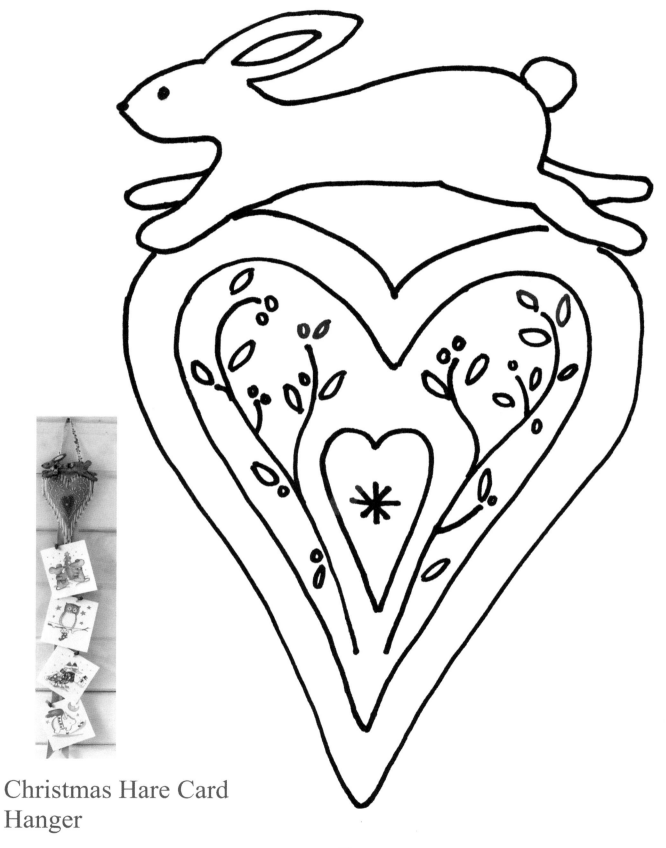

Christmas Hare Card
Hanger

Sparkle Reindeer

ЯЯƎM

ƧIЯНϽ

ƧAMT

Wish upon a Star: Mr Fox

Actual size and both ways round to suit your preferred method of transfer.

Marching Elephants - actual size

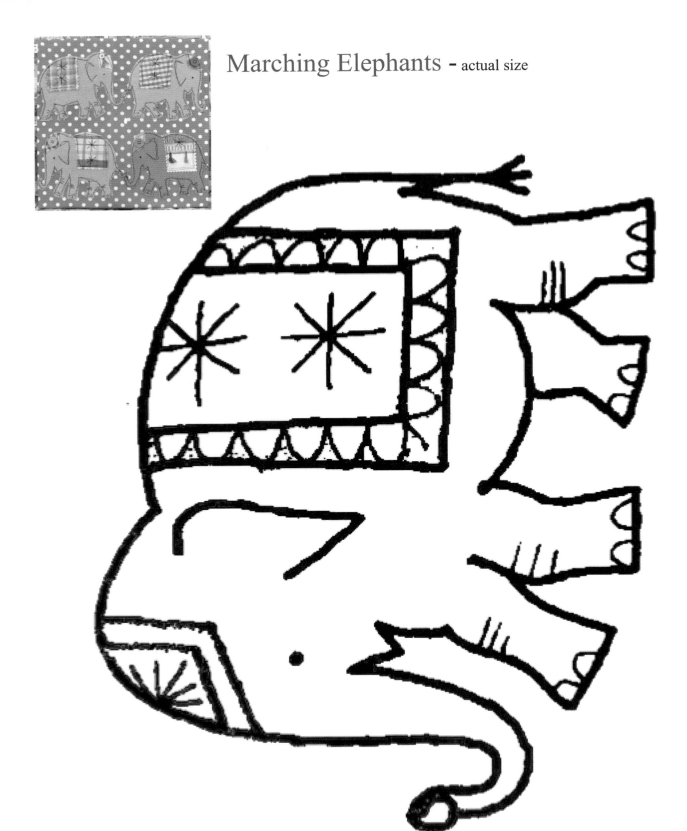

The First Christmas Tree

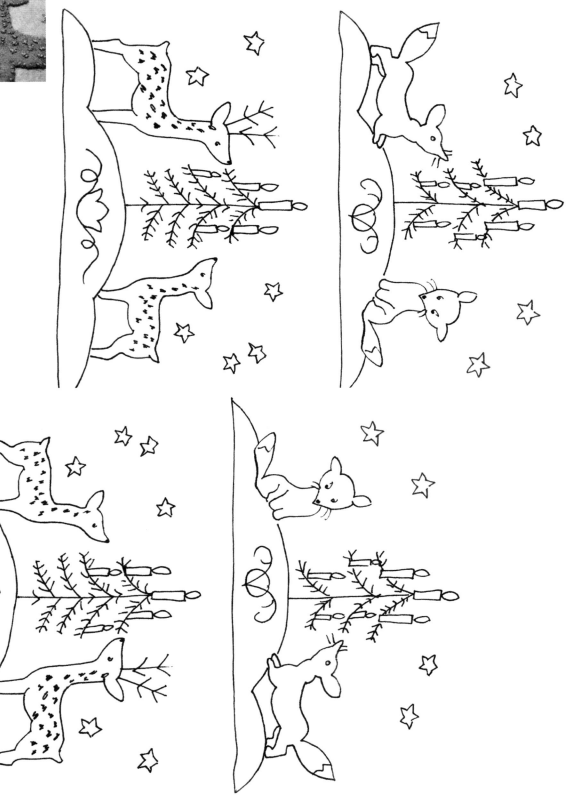

Holly & Berry Baby Reindeer Softie

Actual size

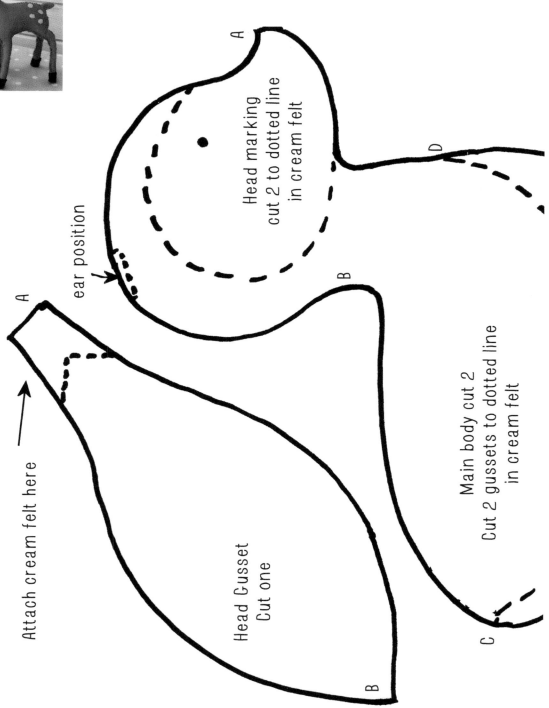

Head marking
cut 2 to dotted line
in cream felt

ear position

Head marking

A

D

B

Main body cut 2
Cut 2 gussets to dotted line
in cream felt

A

Attach cream felt here

Head Gusset
Cut one

B

C

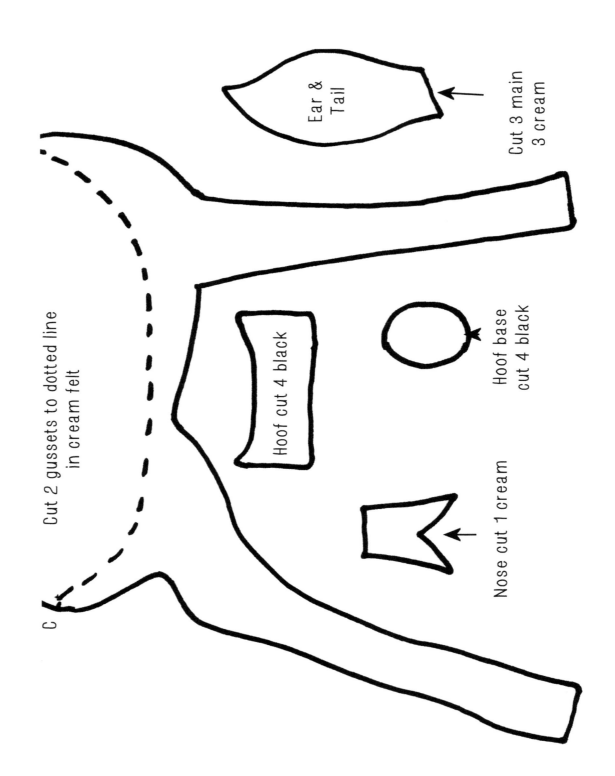

Ear &
Tail

Cut 3 main
3 cream

Cut 2 gussets to dotted line
in cream felt

C

Hoof cut 4 black

Hoof base
cut 4 black

Nose cut 1 cream

Santa Christmas Apron - actual
size and reversed for you to trace onto the paper
side of your Bondaweb

61

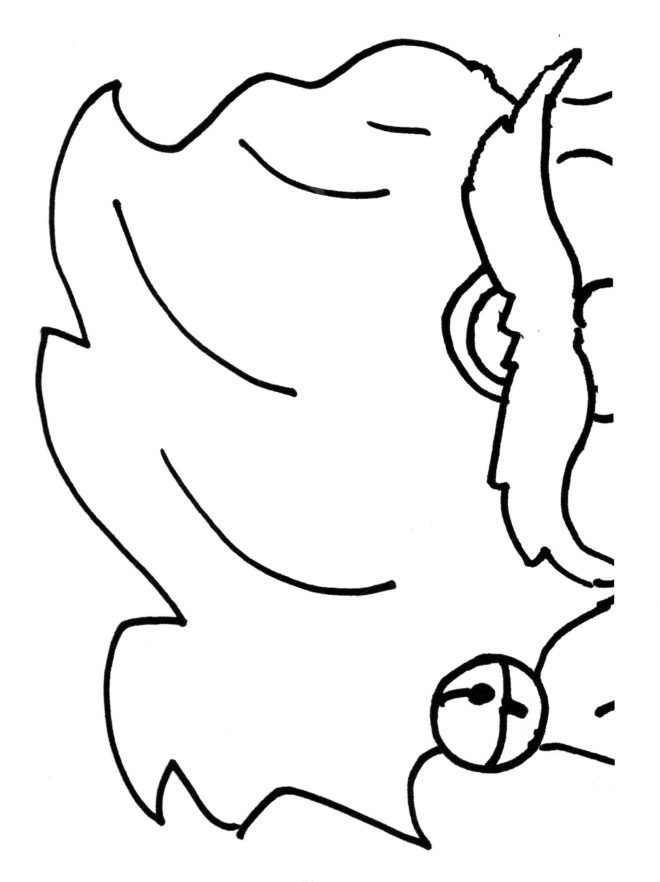

Nativity (actual size)

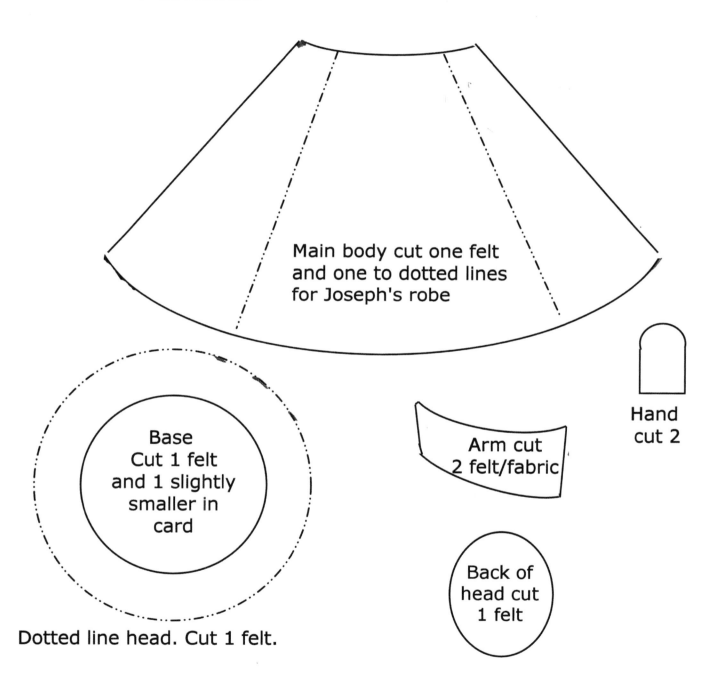

Main body cut one felt
and one to dotted lines
for Joseph's robe

Base
Cut 1 felt
and 1 slightly
smaller in
card

Dotted line head. Cut 1 felt.

Arm cut
2 felt/fabric

Hand
cut 2

Back of
head cut
1 felt

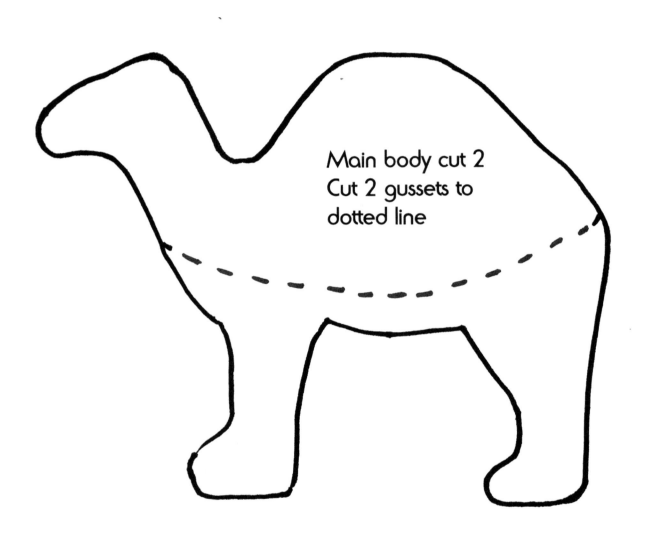

Main body cut 2
Cut 2 gussets to
dotted line